Who's Got the Button?

The

Charm String.

Who's Got the Button?

OLD AND NEW ANGLES
TO BUTTON COLLECTING

by Catherine Roberts

*Illustrated by the author,
and with photographs*

DAVID McKAY COMPANY, Inc.   NEW YORK

WHO'S GOT THE BUTTON

COPYRIGHT © 1962 BY CATHERINE ROBERTS

LIBRARY OF CONGRESS CATALOG CARD NUMBER: 62-18709

MANUFACTURED IN THE UNITED STATES OF AMERICA

VAN REES PRESS   •   NEW YORK

Typography by Charles M. Todd

Acknowledgments

THE AUTHOR wishes to express her appreciation and thanks to the following for their co-operation and courtesy:

Miss Edith Adams, Librarian, The Cooper Union Museum Reference Library, The Cooper Union, New York.

Mrs. Lillian Smith Albert, Hightstown, N. J., author, editor, and leading authority on buttons.

Mr. Calvin S. Hathaway, Director, Museum of the Arts of Decoration, The Cooper Union, for permission to use the photographs of the Fancy Buttons and the Buttons in the 18th Century Costume, from the Museum's collection.

Mrs. Marion Lawson, Pawtucket, R. I., collector, and owner of the modern Pearly Queen costume.

Mr. Harold Van Buren, Brooklyn, New York, collector of military and fraternal buttons, and pin-backs.

Also

Miss Rose Dobbs, editor, David McKay Company, Inc., for being bitten by the button bug.

And

Mr. Edmund P. Roberts, New York, who photographed 12 of the 19 illustrations that embellish *Who's Got the Button?*

Contents

1. Who Collects Buttons, and Why? 1

2. Anecdotes and Tid-bits 13

3. Charm Strings and Pearly Queens 26

4. Today's Specials 35

5. A Suggested Shopping List 45

6. Be a Display Artist 52

7. How to Make Beautiful Buttons 64

8. A Button Time Table 80

9. Goofies, Pin-Backs, and Others 88

   Bibliography 93

   Index 95

LIST OF PHOTOGRAPHS

Between pages 34 and 35

1. A Picture of a Button Garden
   Mounted in Embroidery Hoops

2. Copper Wire and Wooden Mold Buttons

3. Crocheted Buttons

4. Roll-up and Sailor's Knot

5. Embroidered, Ribbon, Hairpin Lace

6. Button Gardens

7. Coins into Buttons

8. Special Collection, French

Between pages 66 and 67

9. Pin-Backs

10. A Pearly Queen Costume

11. Trolley Cars, Fraternals, Defense

12. Buttons of the 19th Century

13. Fancy Buttons

14. Around the World with Buttons

15. Buttons in 18th Century Costume

16. Sporting Buttons

FULL PAGE LINE DRAWINGS

Page

The Charm String .... *Frontispiece*

Mounting Buttons for Display 56

Framing Special Collections and
Fun Fashions 57

Copper Wire 67

Flat Weave and
Chinese Button 72

The Dorset Wheel 73

Designs for Painting and
Embroidering Buttons 76

Who's Got the Button?

Who Collects Buttons, and Why?

W ho collects buttons? Let's see:
... a good many boys who have caught on
to the fact that certain kinds of buttons make tremendously interesting he-man collections that they're proud to show.

... innumerable men who are Civil War buffs, or who are fascinated with the way political history is recorded on campaign buttons.

... 50,000 serious button collectors and dealers.

... all of the leading museums and many small local ones.

... thousands of women who automatically cut the buttons off worn-out garments before throwing them away.

... owners of uncounted numbers of old or large houses whose attics afford storage space for things inherited from Aunt Hattie, Grandma Hayes or Great-aunt Lizzie.

... and you, although maybe you hadn't thought about it.

Everyone is born with a strong instinct to acquire and hoard objects of one kind or another. Little children do it, first with toys and then with things they pick up and stow away in their pockets or bureau drawers.

How many times have you heard some mother wail, "Why on earth do you have to collect all this junk?"

That crazy collection of stuff she digs out and throws away certainly doesn't make sense to her. It probably doesn't to the child, either. Sense really isn't important at this stage. For him, there was a momentary magic in these things. In some way or other they touched his imagination and became valuable and worth treasuring. He might watch his stuff being chucked into the trash can with complete indifference or howl in protest at its disposal. Pretty soon his pockets or bureau will again be jammed with things that didn't make sense.

This hoarding, like that of the old lady in New York who carefully saved and labeled "Pieces of

String, Too Short to Use," is simply a manifestation of an instinct that is as old as man himself.

Between the extremes of the very young and the very old lady lies a vast number of boys and girls, men and women, who *collect* things rather than hoard them. They pick and choose, compare and study the things they collect. Not only that but they always seem to want to tell *you* all about their collection. They want to explain the enchantment and excitement of their particular collection, the reasons why they choose what they do. They want to re-live their adventures and victories in getting this or that particular piece. This is good in more ways than one.

The world is so filled with collectibles and the people to collect them that a listing of the categories would fill a couple of books. For every object you can think of, there is a collector. Many of them are un-consciously so, collectors, I mean. Think of your own home. How many pitchers does your mother have that she seldom if ever uses? Or pieces of costume jewelry? Or teapots? Turn a cold eye on your own possessions. You're a collector too. Everyone is!

The reasons why one chooses this, that or the next thing to collect are as different as the people con-cerned. Mr. Hughes thinks his son Johnny is completely wacky to spend so much of his allowance on old toy train catalogs. Your father thinks Mr. Hughes ought to have his head examined for filling his house with old clocks that don't run. What your mother thinks about Mrs. Smith and the fortune she's put into those old dolls is something you've very wisely kept to yourself.

The really important thing about collecting is not the "why" but the "what."

What do you get out of it?

What does it do for you?

What are its possibilities for continued interest and growth?

What are the rewards you'll gain and victories achieved?

What do you do with it after you've got it?

No one actually sits down and weighs the benefits (the answers to the above questions) of one collection against another. The reason behind a choice of category is usually an emotional one. A thing appeals because it is small and delicate, and you like tiny things. Or, you're mad about anything to do with space, so models of space ships and missiles fill your room. Eventually they take up so much space you switch to something else. But no matter what it is, its interest is enormously increased if it offers you the opportunity to explore and study its background and history. This does not imply that you must be a scholar. You might even hate school work. Actually, all you need to know is how to read.

Take buttons, for instance.

They're small. Compare the space a hundred buttons take up with that needed for the same number of dolls or toy train catalogs. There are hundreds of different kinds of buttons and they can be found every place, starting right with your mother's sewing or button box. They cost practically nothing, especially when compared with the price of some other collectibles. What's more, buttons go so far back in history, are the subject of so many legends and stories, so much fact and fancy, that button research becomes an interesting by-product of button collecting.

Just look at the way the word has slipped into our language. Although it is not as common as it used to be, the phrase, "Aw, button up your lip!" is a slang substitute for the less acceptable "Shut up!"

"He's missing a few buttons" indicates skepticism concerning the sanity or brightness of someone, a remark so easily understood it never needs explaining. Neither does the comment, "She buttonholed me on Main Street and I thought I'd never get away."

A pageboy or bellhop in England is called "Buttons" for obvious reasons, and a bachelor's button is a charming, old-fashioned flower. The buttonwood tree (you may know it as a Carolina sycamore or a London plane tree) comes by its common name for two reasons: its fruit, which hangs on the tree all winter, looks exactly like round, ball-type buttons; and the close-grained, yellowish wood of the tree was used in the manufacture of buttons.

The proper noun "Button," while comparatively rare in this country, was borne by one of the signers of the Declaration of Independence—Button Gwinnet. It was not a nickname but a perfectly ordinary first name in Gloucestershire, England, where he was born in 1735.

After Button Gwinnet came to this country and settled in Savannah, Georgia, in about 1765, he became extremely active politically, serving as delegate to the Second and Third Continental Congress as well as presiding over the Georgia Assembly. In 1777, he was killed in a duel by General Lachlan McIntosh. Of all the "signers" of the Declaration of Independence, Button Gwinnet's autograph commands the highest price because there are so few examples of it.

And talking about duels, a story is told about an "affair of honor" that involved Andrew Jackson, seventh president of the United States. The duel took place between Andrew Jackson and Charles Dickinson, in Tennessee. Both were crack shots although Mr. Dickinson was conceded to be Mr. Jackson's superior. The night before the duel a Mr. Overton, Jackson's best friend, advised him to wear a particular coat having large, heavy silver buttons on it. Naturally, the next morning, Dickinson aimed at the button over Jackson's heart and fired. Jackson fired back, mortally wounding his opponent. Jackson suffered two broken ribs and a severely bruised chest from the impact of Dickinson's bullet against the heavy silver button. But he owed his life to Mr. Overton, who had moved the silver button further over the night before.

"Button, Button, Who's Got the Button?" is the jingle accompanying a game that kindergartners are taught to introduce them to group play. A little later, they learn to chant, "Rich Man, Poor Man, Beggarman, Thief! Doctor, Lawyer, Indian Chief." This fortune-telling game is meaningless unless someone is equipped with enough buttons to count off in sequence. Despite the omnipresent zipper, enough button-wearing candidates help keep this game alive. There is a certain magic in it, a certain unpredictable quality that both delights and amuses.

During non-daisy blooming periods and in areas where that flower is unprocurable, buttons serve to count off, "He loves you, he loves you not." Buttons have also been used in the game of checkers and in various forms of hopscotch.

The forerunner of our game, Pitching Pennies, was played in England during the last part of the nineteenth century. Fairly large, flat brass buttons, known as "bangers," were used exactly as pennies are used in our game. The players had a variation called "On the Line," in which bangers were lined up and a "nicker"—a much larger coachman's button—was used to knock as many off the line as possible in one throw.

English boys also carried on a lively trade in buttons. Attaching specific values and names to various types, an accepted form of exchange that was strictly adhered to, they collected buttons from old clothes, graded them, and did a thriving business. Like almost anything else, commonness or rarity influenced the buttons' trading value.

"Sinkeys," a concave metal button with holes for sewing, were "one-ers." "Shankeys," a self-evident bit of nomenclature, were either "two-ers" or "three-ers," depending on size, beauty or unusualness. Real prizes, having a higher valuation, were "Liveries." These were metal buttons from the uniforms of servants. They were either lettered or bore heraldic devices and were rated as "three-ers," "four-ers," or "five-ers." Best of all were the "six-ers," large bronze affairs bearing sporting devices: foxes, birds, deer, symbols of various sports, etc.

In the old days, Scotch warriors wore heavy, diamond-shaped silver buttons on their kilts for one purpose only—to assure them of a proper burial if they were killed on foreign soil. The value of the buttons was figured to cover the cost involved. Diamond-shaped silver buttons still appear on Highland dress although their original purpose no longer exists.

Today, a man's dress or morning coat always has two small, silk-covered buttons at the waistline in back. This is a holdover from the days in the last century when all men wore tail coats for ordinary wear and rode horseback. These two little buttons were used to hold up the tails while riding. The convention of having buttons on the lower sleeves of a man's sports or suit jacket harks back to the days when buttons were placed there for the specific purpose of allowing the sleeve to be opened and turned back in order to reveal the fine lace-trimmed linen shirt sleeve.

The linen shirt became a mark of distinction as early as 945 A.D. None but the wealthy could afford good linen, which is why men's vests and coats never button up tightly to the neck. They were originally cut away to expose the fine linen shirt which later was embellished with ruffles and frills.

For a long time there was no rule concerning on which side a male or female garment should button. Either from right to left or left to right was a matter of personal choice or the whim of the dressmaker or tailor. As soon as men began wearing swords as part of everyday as well as military dress, their garments were always buttoned from left to right to eliminate the awkward openings and edges that the sword hilt might catch in. Like today's TV Westerner, a swordsman had to have a fast draw.

The traditional Chinese gown always has five buttons on it—to remind the wearer of the five great virtues emphasized by Confucius: Justice, Humility, Order, Prudence, and Rectitude.

Three centuries ago, the Puritans in England, revolted by the extravagance both in the size and richness of buttons, shunned them completely. They used hooks and eyes, as do many of the present-day Amish people in this country, to illustrate their disapproval of "vanities." The original gesture soon became mandatory and offenders were brought before the church council for correction.

It is said that pearls and diamonds, as well as secret messages, were smuggled across frontiers in dome-shaped buttons. Their hollow tops could be twisted off, providing a fair amount of space to hide small objects. That could be true. Similar buttons were made for the specific purpose of carrying small wads of perfume-soaked cotton. The domes, which also twisted off to allow replacing old wads, were perforated so that the perfume could escape.

Within the past two years some modern twist-apart buttons have been found whose purpose was to conceal poison. Looking exactly like ordinary Army Issue (both American and Canadian) uniform buttons, their slightly domed tops could be opened. It is believed that these were issued to special commando outfits. The poison probably was for personal use in case of torture. Maybe that was the true function of the button. Maybe not. Either way, it offers interesting speculation.

The way this small object has slipped into so many and varied aspects of life is truly astonishing. At a very early stage, it combined the functional with the decorative. It has been used to designate various social, professional, and economic ranks. It has been responsible for important inventions and the founding of equally important industries. Fortunes have been made and lost through buttons, and lives have been saved by them—as was President Jackson's.

Every art and craft has been employed in making buttons: painting, sculpture, goldsmithing, metal working, pottery, ceramic and glass-blowing and molding, die cutting and stamping and the needle skills. All have played major roles in the making of buttons.

Every material known to man, natural and synthetic, has been transformed into buttons. All the metals—precious, base, and alloys; wood, bone, shell, leather, silk, cotton, clay, feathers; insects; nuts, seeds, linen, pits, papier-mâché; precious stones and gems, common stones, horn, rubber, gutta-percha, celluloid and modern synthetics; wires, threads, cord, coal, and petrified materials. Can you name anything else? If so, the chances are that it too has been used for buttons.

Poets have rhymed and rebus-writers have rebused for the button trade. A late nineteenth century poet enjoyed modest fame during his lifetime but the only example of his work that is still commonly known is a four-line verse which goes like this:

> Old Grimes is dead, that good old man,
> We ne'er shall see him more.
> He used to wear an old black coat,
> All buttoned down before.

Anecdotes and Tid-bits

Ancient peoples, living around the eastern end of the Mediterranean Sea, achieved exceedingly high levels of culture and civilization. Their jewelry was extraordinarily beautiful, showing great artistic and technical skill as well as lovely and sophisticated designs. Yet, they held their garments together with fibulae (pins), clasps, belts and girdles, ties and cords. You'd think that people as smart as that would have caught on to the simplicity and effectiveness of a minor device such as the button. But they didn't.

Many of their rosette or disk-shaped fibulae have been mistaken for buttons, as were the glass beads found in ancient Egyptian tombs. Weather and climate may have had something to do with this strange oversight. For the most part their garments were flowing, draped, loose, not requiring tight fit for protection and comfort.

What is a button?

Fundamentally, it's a knob or disk that is attached to a garment to close or fasten it by passing through a loop or slit (buttonhole).

The first real button was found in about 1865 in a Danish peat bog during archaeological excavations. Buttons, fibulae, woven clothing, reed baskets, wood rakes were dug from a barrow in Schleswig, Denmark, in a remarkable state of preservation. All iron articles had disintegrated but the peat had preserved everything else. These finds are dated by the experts as having been used during Denmark's Early Iron Age, 250 B.C. to 45 A.D.

The climate of Denmark, Northern Germany and Holland required snugly fitted clothes. Trousers, both short and long, and some with attached feet; long and short sleeved shirts; capes, hoods, cloaks—all made of woven wool, leather and fur—were the Barbarians' style of clothing. During this same period, southern peoples were going around in lightweight fabrics and near nakedness.

There is no real evidence of buttons having been commonly used in Europe until the beginning of the eleventh century. To claim that they were in use then is begging the question.

The only evidence to support belief in such an early date lies in the illustrations of missals, hymn books and manuscripts. An alert eye can easily pick out what looks like buttons in those old, fairly crude drawings. But what looks like buttons could also be an over-simplified representation of embroidery, which was used for trimming in those days.

There is no evidence of the use of buttons in the church sculpture of the period, a most reliable source of costume history. Churches of any size, particularly those in fairly important cities, were decorated both inside and out with tremendous numbers of statues. While the statues represented saints who had died hundreds of years earlier, the stone carvers often dressed them in the style of clothes being worn by themselves and their townspeople. The carvings are extremely detailed, and if buttons had been worn at the time they would have been included.

From the eleventh century on, the history of buttons is quite fascinating. There are long periods wherein the button is relegated to an inconspicuous, purely functional role. Other periods use buttons so lavishly that wearing the garments they decorated must have been quite a feat. In many cases, the help of an abacus is almost necessary to get an accurate count of the buttons used on a single garment. This is particularly true of men's costumes. During many periods they were a good deal fancier than women's clothes. (See Photograph No. 15.)

Royalty and the nobility, of course, went way out in their use of buttons. They also took steps to try to prevent ordinary people from copying their fashions. In the twelfth century fines were levied on townswomen who dressed as richly as noblewomen. The records show that they paid their fines—if they couldn't talk their way out of them—and continued to dress just as richly.

In 1290 A.D., Queen Elinor, wife of Edward I of England, attended her sister's wedding in a dress that had been renovated for the occasion. It is on record that this gown was trimmed with 636 silver buttons! Even quite small ones would have made that a fairly heavy load to carry around. A quarter of a century later, a woman's cloak might have as many as fifty buttons on it, while her husband's doublet and cloak sported eighty or more.

It always took some time before ordinary people adopted the court fashions. A great middle class was developing. Townspeople were accumulating substantial fortunes and using a goodly part of them in personal adornment. Rich fabrics and furs, splendid jewelry and buttons, extravagantly embroidered accessories, and dazzling hats and shoes were no longer the exclusive prerogative of royalty and nobility. Many laws were drawn up in an effort to curtail and control this extravagance among the middle class. But it is one thing to pass a law and quite another to enforce it.

The difficulties administrators of those laws experienced are revealed in the following actual record in Florence, Italy, as reported by one of the administrators under Giovanni di Bicci (1360-1428 A.D.):

"When, obeying the orders you gave me, I went out to seek for the forbidden ornaments of your women, they met me with arguments such as are not to be found in any book of laws. There cometh a woman with the peak of her hood fringed out and twined about her head. My notary sayeth, 'Tell me your name, for you have a peak with fringes.' Then the good woman taketh this peak, which is fastened around her hood with a pin, and, holding it in her hand, she declareth that it is a wreath. Then going further he findeth one wearing many buttons in front of her dress, and he saith to her, 'Ye are not allowed to wear these buttons.' But she answers, 'These are not buttons but studs, and if ye do not believe me, look . . . they have no loops, and moreover there are no buttonholes.' Then my notary goeth to another who is wearing ermine, and saith, 'Now what can she say to this? Ye are wearing ermine.' And he prepares to write down her name. But the woman answers, 'Do not write me down, for this is not ermine, it is the fur of a suckling.' Saith the notary, 'What is this suckling?' And the woman replies, 'It is an animal.' "

Needless to say, that particular administrator as well as hundreds like him, threw up their hands in despair.

Most of the sumptuary laws were devised in an attempt to regulate business and finance so that a nation might grow and develop its resources and industries. Various Acts of the English Parliament, from the time of William and Mary to George I, forbade the wearing of cloth-covered buttons. The purpose of these acts was to create and encourage a market for metal buttons, a new industry that showed great possibilities for growth and importance in the national economy.

It became obvious that no government could effectively impose any such regulations. As soon as those restrictions were allowed to fade away, the thing they were trying to achieve occurred automatically. Fashions changed and the simple little cloth-covered button was replaced by all sorts of metal buttons, many of them of great beauty and richness.

By the eighteenth century, the wearing of buttons made of precious metals and jewels was so common that highway robbers and footpads carried razors with which to "bubble" their victims; i.e., slash off their buttons. This was a far more profitable form of theft than stealing the purses of wealthy gentry. Gentlemen did not carry much, if any money, with them.

In the same century, government patents were issued for various ways of manufacturing the component parts of buttons. The improvements and inventions of new machines for this purpose opened the way to important new methods of manufacturing other items. At the same time, experiments with new materials for making buttons introduced these same materials into other fields.

The valuable process of vulcanizing rubber was discovered by button makers. They also perfected a method of silver plating on copper that was called English Plate. The method was quickly adapted by the manufacturers of table and decorative silverware and is known today as Sheffield plate. The birth of the vastly important brass industries in New England was a direct outcome of the great demand for buttons.

Of course, while all of this was going on, the handmade and the homemade button was being produced in enormous quantities. Goldsmiths and jewelers, glass and ceramic workers, embroiderers and weavers were using their talents and skills to make buttons.

East Dorset, England, was a village whose prosperity was entirely dependent upon a specific type of button. Nearly a thousand people were employed in this cottage industry; their products were exported to all parts of Europe and America. The Dorset Button was first made of disks cut from sheep horn and covered with cloth. These were called High Tops. Other styles were worked out and given such names as Bird's Eye, Yarrell, Old Dorset, Honeycomb, Basket, Carolus, Singleton and Crosswheel. Of them all, the technique of making the Dorset Wheel is the only one that has survived. This is a particularly charming and distinctive style of button and one that is easily made with a needle and thread. (See illustration on page 73.)

In 1860, a button-making machine, invented by John Ashton, literally killed the Dorset Button industry. The cost of handmade buttons, low as it was, could not compete with that of machine-made ones. Almost overnight, this cottage industry was wiped out.

Much of the story and history of buttons lies buried in old documents, wills, diaries, letters, laundry lists, inventories, advertisements, bills, shopping lists and newspaper accounts of the costumes worn by royalty or other prominent people.

The London *Daily Post*, March 3, 1730, reports: "His Majesty had a vastly rich suit, the buttons on his coat being of diamonds, every one worth, it is said, £250."

There were frequent advertisements for Lost,

Found or Stolen Articles in which the identifying features were buttons:

February 24, 1680: *Domestic Intelligence*—"Found: a campaign coat with plate buttons."

October 12, 1676: London *Gazette*—"A servant hath stolen one velvet coat with plate buttons; one set of plate buttons newly boyled, one suit of grey clothes with gilt brass buttons."

Following the death of a dry-goods merchant in England, a "Trewe and perfect inventory of the goods and chattels of Thomas Cowcher of the Cittie Worcester, Mercer [cloth merchant], lately deceased, taken, viewed and prised, 14th daye November, Anno Domini 1643 . . . by William Gough". . . . found that Cowcher's stock included over six thousand buttons. That's a sizeable inventory for just one merchant in a not very large city.

In the same century, Samuel Pepys, the great English diarist writes (1659) . . . "this morning came home my fine camlett cloak with gold buttons and a silk suit which cost me much money." Five days later he writes: "This morning my brother Tom brought me my Jackanapes coat with the silver buttons." Since camlett was a very costly material woven of camel's hair and silk, it is obvious that Mr. Pepys was both well-to-do and a dandy.

Until comparatively recently, children's clothes were

miniature editions of those worn by adults. They, too, bore their burden of buttons, reflecting the fashions of their time. Early American and English portraits of children illustrate this point effectively. They also prove that this period—the seventeenth, eighteenth and early nineteenth centuries—was a high point in the masculine use of buttons. However, social and national upheavals and changes were influencing modes of dress and the accessories worn with them.

The American Revolution not only cut off the European market but it also curtailed the provincial manufacture of metal buttons. Sobriety of dress naturally follows a period of national crisis. Rich fabrics, embroideries and laces, fancy buttons and jewelry were put aside and forgotten. It was patriotic to wear home produced fabrics and these were buttoned with natural, easily obtained materials such as horn, wood, bone, and shell, as well as the unique fabrications ingenious women concocted for the purpose.

The flow of imported buttons following the Revolution was again stopped during the War of 1812. This shortage provided the greatest impetus to American manufacturing of buttons, particularly metal ones. Military uniforms, to which people had become accustomed during the American and French revolutions and the rise of Bonapartism, influenced men's fashions.

Metal buttons, therefore, became highly desirable and were used with a lavish hand.

But it was a different story with women's fashions.

Here, the most outstanding characteristic of the first two decades of the nineteenth century was the straight, almost tubular gown that all females wore. Holding these gowns on the figure depended upon two drawstrings—one at the neck which was usually quite low, and the other directly under the bosom. There was little call for buttons until the switch from the tubular silhouette to the tight basque and very full skirt, a style that started in the 1830's, brought buttons back, both as a functional and a decorative accessory.

The importation of fancy buttons from Europe increased. China buttons, printed with small colorful motifs that duplicated the patterns of the popular calicos, became extremely popular. They are just as popular today with collectors and are much sought after. (See Photograph No. 13.)

The potential market in America was sufficiently attractive to European manufacturers to induce them to participate in the New York Exhibition of Industry in 1852.

Stimulated by the success of the British Exhibition, New York City built its own Crystal Palace on the site of the present Bryant Park, an area bounded by

Forty and Forty-second streets and by the Avenue of the Americas. Its eastern boundary was the Croton Distributing Reservoir, now the site of the New York Public Library. Among the many foreign and domestic exhibits were those of fancy buttons from Bavaria, Silesia, Saxe-Altenburg, Rhenish Prussia, Austria, and France.

By the 1860's, there was little doubt about the importance of buttons in the United States.

Women's gowns and coats flaunted from 60 to 108 buttons on a single garment. A little girl's dress, pictured in the January, 1861 issue of *Godey's Ladies' Book*, showed 88 drop buttons. Boys' costumes were equally well endowed, making up in size what they didn't have in numbers.

Papa, too, went about his business liberally bedecked with buttons, although they were inconspicuous in color if not in size and numbers. By the turn of the twentieth century, buttons for masculine wear had become purely functional.

World War I precipitated an almost total eclipse of buttons, both functionally and decoratively. While they had lost status from a fashion point of view, buttons were still absolutely necessary for many types of clothing. They fought a long, drawn-out and successful battle against being completely supplanted by slide fasteners. By 1937, the wholesale value of buttons being manufactured amounted to $31,000,000 a year.

With the recent fashion emphasis, twenty-five years later, the role of buttons has orbited almost beyond calculation. Modern manufacturing methods and new materials are contributing enormously to this fashion emphasis. Aside from the manufactured buttons, the variety of which is astounding, handmade buttons are quite as important in the style picture. Handmade buttons are imported from Germany and other European countries. They are also being made in this country by private individuals, and they compete quite successfully with the finest that is being brought in from abroad.

The mid-twentieth century button is the collector's button of the future, and the future is not very far off.

Charm Strings and Pearly Queens

The first formal button collectors in this country were young girls of the mid- and late-Victorian periods. The key word, "collector," is apt because it means gathering examples of an item for a purpose other than the original one for which it was designed. That sounds more complicated than it actually is.

Button saving, as testified to by innumerable button boxes, was and is motivated by the thrift instinct most women possess. A garment would wear out but the chances were that its buttons were still good and could be used again. So, into the button box they went. A large percentage never got out again until some collector came along and poked around in the box.

The first collectors were the Victorian girls who assembled Charm Strings. Their goal was to acquire 999 buttons, preferably before their friends did. Ideally, each button should be different and be a present from someone. Trading was allowed, but not buying. Duplicates, of course, appeared but they were subject to criticism and scorn. The thousandth button was to be avoided at all costs. Accidentally acquiring it would doom its collector to spinsterhood!

Telling off the buttons of one's Charm String kept rivalry alive and permitted of a little bragging. "Aunt Lillie gave me this one from a dress she wore attending the Inaugural Ball in Washington." "Old Mrs. Gray told me that this one came off her grandfather's uniform." "May Whitney traded me this one for that old calico one you gave me."

It was a pleasant way to spend a summer afternoon, particularly when one was allowed to root through mother's or grandmother's button box. Many Charm Strings found their way back into button boxes as interest in them waned when new and more exciting hobbies arose. To find an original Charm String today would be a wonderful piece of luck because most of them have been broken up or thrown away.

While Victorian girls were putting together their Charm Strings, another button collection was being assembled by a man who had served his country through the Civil War—Captain Luis Fenolosa Emilio.

Captain Emilio had inherited a few Revolutionary buttons, and occasionally picked up other military buttons. In 1887, his casual interest was sharpened by an article in a Philadelphia newspaper, written by George Norton Galloway. It interested Captain Emilio sufficiently to inspire him to go to Philadelphia and meet the author. Captain Emilio described Mr. Galloway as being . . . "a large man, with a deep voice, of friendly manner and curiously interesting, for he had been a soldier, singer, actor, writer, and was a collector of buttons." Obviously, this description was motivated by Captain Emilio's desire to prove that a man collecting buttons was not necessarily a sissy.

Just as obviously, Mr. Galloway stimulated Captain Emilio to begin a serious search for military buttons. In fact, he spent the rest of his life on the lookout for examples to add to his collection. The collection, which is most comprehensive and important, is now in the Essex Institute, Salem, Massachusetts. Its size and completeness are only fully appreciated when one remembers the difficulties entailed in assembling it.

There were no dealers in old buttons to whom the captain might go to secure a desired item. Neither were there newspaper columns or hobby magazines through which he might get co-operation and information. No societies or clubs existed that might be of help. His was a lone search. It led him to curio and antique stores, tailor shops, and second-hand clothes dealers, both here and abroad. It involved an enormous amount of correspondence and became a life-time project.

His book, *The Emilio Collection of Military Buttons*, printed in 1911, is constantly referred to for information and authentication by the tremendous number of present-day collectors of military buttons.

True, Captain Emilio had the field to himself and could therefore assemble a unique collection. His vision in doing so is equally unique. But the opportunities of parallelling his accomplishment are just as possible today. His collection includes buttons from 1780 to 1904. There has been considerable military activity since then.

David F. Johnson's 2–volume work, *Uniform Buttons of the American Armed Forces*, (1784–1948), provides comprehensive reference material for the collector of modern military buttons. Volume 1 is exclusively descriptions, while Volume 2 contains the photographs that illustrate the descriptions.

The use of buttons in political campaigns in this country goes back to the eighteenth century. The first one is the 1789 George Washington silver button bearing the legend "Long Live the President." This is surrounded by a wreath, the loops of which enclose the initials of the original thirteen states. Its scarcity and value is such that counterfeits of it crop up every now and then. However, a facsimile issued as a Centennial button in 1889 is not counterfeit.

Improved methods of casting, embossing and stamping gave rise to substantial issues of buttons designed exclusively for political campaigns. In writing about the "Anti-Whig Campaign Buttons of 1840," in the ' National Button Society's *Bulletin,* (May, 1944), Judge Chester Pendleton reveals how he learned the origin of "O. K."

Political parades and rallies were exciting, colorful and noisy in those days. Drums, bands and whistles accompanied the large floats that touted the virtues and desirability of specific candidates. During the presidential campaign of General William Henry Harrison, a parade in his honor, designed to drum up support, took place on September 15, 1840 in Urbana, Champaign County, Ohio. One of the picturesque floats flaunted a large banner proclaiming:

THE PEOPLE IS OLL KORRECT

General Harrison, incidentally, won, and was inaugurated on March 4, 1841, but unfortunately he died one month later of pneumonia.

Every time there was a political or social upheaval in America, England or France, buttons appeared that reflected the sentiments of the common man. It was

"Up with . . ." and "Down with. . . ." Witty and malicious allegations appeared on buttons to show where the wearer stood on certain issues and to help convert others to the "right" party.

Between these dramatic periods, the simpler and gentler motto button and the rebus type of button were popular. The early motto buttons, made of silver and ceramic, were often very beautiful. Sentimental legends such as "Calm in the midst of storms" . . . "No roses without tears" . . . "Even the most watchful is deceived" were daintily lettered on the face of fairly generous sized buttons.

Rebuses, of course, were ingenious combinations of symbols, letters and words. The trick was to use as few words as possible to get the message across. For instance, if you wanted to say, "My eye is on you," the only word would be "my" followed by the drawing of an eye superimposed on the letter U.

During the last part of the nineteenth century, an amusing group of buttons, called the "Road to Ruin," were most popular. These were of glass (backed with metal) and had inset designs showing the traditional symbols of wine, women, song, racing and gambling. They were used on men's waistcoats and jackets and appeared on the Costermonger costumes of the late 80's and 90's.

The Costermongers certainly knew what to do with

the contents of an old button box. If you have ever rooted through such a box you'll remember that about 90 per cent of its contents are small to medium size pearl buttons from children's clothing, men's shirts, etc. This is just as true in England as it is here.

The fruit and vegetable vendors in London, called Costermongers, have always been interested in helping the poor. They did this by yearly drives to raise money for the hospitals in their areas. Back in the late eighties, one Henry Croft dreamed up the idea that a gay, costumed parade would catch the public's attention and stimulate interest in this charitable work.

Taking his everyday suit—bell-bottomed trousers, short, square cut jacket, bright scarf at the throat, and a bowler (which we call a derby)—he trimmed it lavishly with complicated designs and patterns worked out entirely in pearl buttons. The effect was brilliant, so the same thing was done on his wife's dress which, if you remember costume history, fitted tightly through the body and then swept down to the ground with considerable fullness. The dress was literally covered with ornate pearl button designs. To top it off, Mrs. Croft wore a tremendous velvet hat trimmed with six or more giddy ostrich plumes.

Other leaders of Costermonger districts made similar costumes, and thus were born the Pearlie Kings and the Pearlie Queens, a tradition which is still in existence. While style changes have crept into the basic garments—skirts are shorter and trousers are straight—the same elaborate patterning of pearl buttons is maintained. The spelling of the name has also changed to Pearly. You can imagine the weight of one of these outfits when you realize that over 30,000 buttons are used on a single garment.

Today, the annual Costermongers' campaign is held to raise money for television sets for the hospitals serving London's poor. Their parade is just as giddy and glittering as it was seventy years ago and the Pearly costumes make a rabid button collector itch to do a little bubbling of his own. (See Photograph No. 10.)

Interestingly enough, these Pearly costumes are not put away from one year to the next. They are worn with pride by their owners on week ends at the races or at other parades or any place where there are large gatherings of people. If there are children in the family, they too appear in Pearly outfits and are designated "Prince" or "Princess," as the case may be.

Long before there was any organized or systematized collecting of buttons, people were intrigued by the information, beauty and interest they provided. Even the most casual study revealed strange, important or historically significant data that piqued the curiosity and inspired subsequent research. Interest in buttons grew with astonishing strength and rapidity.

Groups and assortments of buttons kept cropping up at antique shows, hobby displays and exhibitions. Unlike furniture or glassware or silver, no standards existed for buttons. They just kept appearing in ever increasing numbers—but from where?

1. A Picture of a Button Garden Mounted in Embroidery Hoops

A gay little button garden to hang on the wall is easily made with poster paint, rickrack tape and a variety of pearl buttons. Embroidery hoops frame the composition.

2. Copper Wire and Wooden Mold Buttons

Wooden button molds may be decorated with 14 gauge copper wire coiled as fancy dictates. Clear nail polish prevents tarnishing.

3. Crocheted Buttons

Any thread, cord, fibre or yarn that can be crocheted can be used to cover buttons. Metal or wooden molds provide firm shape.

4. Roll-up and Sailor's Knot

Rolled up fabric and woven cord are two of the oldest ways
of making buttons at home. They are high fashion today.

5. Embroidered, Ribbon, Hairpin Lace

Hand embroidery, decorative ribbon and hairpin lace produce handsome buttons for personal use and unusual gifts.

6. Button Gardens

Real gardens that actually grow. Tiny cacti and succulents
planted in large buttons, watered with an eye dropper.

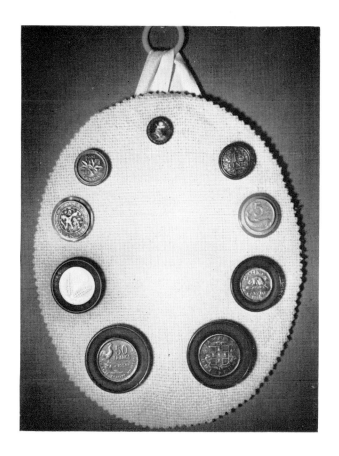

7. Coins Into Buttons

Foreign coins cemented to plain plastic buttons are practical for wear as well as for making up effective wall decorations, for home or classroom.

8. Special Collection, French

Souvenir of a foreign vacation: beautiful
buttons mounted and framed. Insignia
serves to identify place of purchase.

Today's Specials

Fine antique furniture, glassware, decorative accessories, jewelry and embroideries have always had devoted collectors. Following the depression years of the nineteen-thirties, a tremendous number of young people became interested in a class of antiques now called Americana; i.e., pine and maple furniture, pressed glass dishes and table accessories, and old-fashioned china. This was probably due to the fact that these things were, at the time, sold as second-hand articles and were considerably less expensive than modern new furniture and accessories.

Naturally, where there is a market there is going to be people working to supply that market. Favorite sources of supply were farmhouses and shabby old city houses. Some dealers just bought single pieces, while others bought the entire contents of a house, an attic, a barn or carriage shed.

During the process of sorting and evaluating these miscellaneous purchases, thousands of hoards of buttons turned up—in mason jars, shoe boxes, sewing baskets, bowls and vases, flour sacks, sewing machine drawers and fancy candy boxes. Anyone interested in buttons then had a field day. Buttons could be bought by the pound, the box or the jar for practically pennies.

It didn't take dealers long to catch on to the fact that there was something more to buttons than just buttons. They began to sort and separate them. They were put on sale in poke boxes at five and ten cents a button. Many dealers went even further and tried to get some real information. So many people were asking for and buying buttons that there simply had to be something to this new hobby beyond just a passing interest.

Something had to be done about classifying buttons along lines that everyone could recognize and that would serve as standards for judging them at displays and exhibitions.

The National Button Society was organized in 1938 to do just that—clarify, organize and classify the tremendous field of buttons. The obvious and simplest method of getting order out of chaos was to separate buttons into groups determined by the materials of which they were made. With no effort at all you can tick off the major materials, but what happens when a button is made of two or more materials, such as a metal back with a painted glass front? Or an ivory button with a metal inset? Multiply those two problems thousands of times and you will get an idea of the gargantuan job that faced the Society.

The 1962 classifications of buttons as set by the National Button Society includes 7 major divisions having 60 sections and 646 classes. You may never want to enter a Button Show (then again, you might! Who can tell?) but a study of the Classification List will help you classify and identify the buttons you've already acquired. Maybe they're just buttons you've saved from discarded garments or ones you bought because they were so pretty you couldn't pass them up. It will probably surprise you to see what a large division is devoted to modern buttons.

The moderns are broken down into Conventional Shapes and Realistics (goofies) and include Overall Buttons! But you won't find pin-backs. These are not accepted by the Society—yet.

Thousands of adults as well as young people collect pin-backs seriously and persistently. There's a lively trade in them all over the country. They are just as interesting as their more precious cousins, the nineteenth century campaign buttons, and will increase in importance in direct ratio to their age. So get out that box of pin-backs you stowed away because it was kid stuff. Set up your own classifications and keep your weather eye peeled for new ones.

Your present passion may be centered entirely on collecting early Ives or Lionel electric engines, cars and equipment. Or maybe it's early toy train catalogs or HO gauge stuff. Think big and supplement those collections with buttons. Railroad uniform buttons to match the period and/or the name of the line (Santa Fé, Great Western, etc.) are not too hard to come by. There are engineer's buttons, those worn by Pullman car conductors and porters, as well as yard workers and signal tower men. They all have distinctive designs and, when mounted, make very good-looking and interesting accompaniments to your major collection.

Collecting old automobiles is a somewhat limited operation although it is being done. But collecting old advertisements, sales folders, manuals and pictures, as well as books about old cars is enormously entertaining and very widespread. There are quite a number of metal buttons, usually brass, depicting early automobiles, because it was fashionable at the beginning of the century to wear linen dusters (long coats) closed with these buttons. A couple of early automobile ads, combined with one or two matching buttons, makes a very attractive wall decoration. It will also serve to catch people's interest, thereby giving you a perfect excuse to buttonhole them with the rest of the collection.

Just stamps or just buttons leave a good many of us cold. But buttons plus stamps offer one of the most exciting combinations for collectors to assemble. No matter how you look at either, you come up with a new idea. For every commemorative stamp issued you'll find, with some looking, a button bearing a similar design or one so close to it that the two—stamp and button—become bosom companions.

Take air mail stamps and airplane buttons. A two-way operation can be worked; a particularly handsome stamp can be surrounded with buttons, or vice versa. Foreign stamps are especially rich in the possibilities they offer along these lines.

In this age of foreign travel everyone knows someone who is going abroad. A button and a stamp from every foreign country visited makes a valuable and special little collection of great interest.

One enterprising young collector put the proposition this way:

"Gee, Aunt Jane, there's only one thing I think I'd like you to get me in Europe—something that's sorta hard to get over here. You're going to be sending letters and postcards home, so why don't you buy a couple of extra stamps each time—y'know, fancy ones

—and stick them in an envelope for me. Then, when you're shopping, you could look for buttons that sorta matched the stamps. Only don't forget to mark the buttons some way so I'll know what countries they came from. It would be real swell if you could do that!"

Aunt Jane did, and got bitten by the button bug herself!

Mounted insects, real ones, are often quite beautiful. Every common insect you ever heard of has a duplicate in the button world. It's a lot easier for young entomologists to collect button specimens than real insects. A single beetle can be dramatized by surrounding it with various beetle buttons in a wide variety of sizes, shapes and materials. Handsome color photographs, if you bog down at using real insects, can be easily acquired from nature magazines and old copies of the *National Geographic*. The latter is a veritable storehouse of ideas for button collectors.

More ideas will pop if you examine the button exhibits at hobby, antique and button shows. Look particularly for trays of modern buttons that are classified as realistics or goofies. Match them up with similar shapes that are sold for charm bracelets. This is something that's easy and fun to specialize in. See how many musical instruments you can collect, or fruits, vegetables, tools or animals. You can wear the charms on your wrist and the buttons on your sweaters. In the fashion world this is known as co-ordinating one's accessories, and it's a pretty good trick.

With this kind of button collecting you can mix up various classifications to suit your fancy. The variety of materials of which buttons are made frequently makes these little special collections more dramatic.

The trick is to have a specific idea. Then give it some thought. Don't discard an idea because at first it seems crazy or unworkable. Think some more about it and you'll come up with something unusual.

Maybe you are so tied up with a 4-H sheep project right now that you dream, eat, sleep, exist for it alone. Stretch your mind just a little bit. Collect sheep buttons. Wear them on your belt or hatband, your cardigan or pocket flaps. When you win that First Place Ribbon, frame it surrounded with the choicest buttons from your collection.

The cost of this kind of button collecting is practically nothing. If you do have to buy any buttons, remember that a double malted or a banana split costs a lot more! When word gets around about your project you'll be surprised at how many people will offer you buttons for free. Button collectors usually have duplicates or patterns and designs that they don't particularly want or can use. They'll gift you or trade you if they know you are really interested and have a special goal, or they'll put you in touch with someone who can supply the button you're after.

Run your eye over the list below. Everything on it has a button duplicate or a design closely allied to it. This is the material from which special collections are built.

BUTTONS WITH STAMPS . . .

bearing designs of animals

birds	people
musical instruments	agricultural motifs
flowers	conservation motifs
sports	boats, etc.

BUTTONS WITH VALENTINES . . .

cupids	hearts
bows and arrows	mottos
comic figures	flowers, etc.

BUTTONS WITH BUGS . . .

actual or picture of

beetles	bees
butterflies	horse flies
wasps	moths, etc.

BUTTONS WITH CHARMS . . . almost every gold, silver or plastic charm has a counterpart in the button world. There are so many that one *has* to specialize.

Buttons with Coins ... American, English and foreign coins all have design motifs that can be duplicated or approximated with buttons. Indian head, buffalo, tulip tree and oak sprays, eagle, etc.

Buttons with Newspaper Headlines ... a most interesting combination for pin-backs showing portraits or slogans of political campaigns. Ditto missile and space activities (Shepard and Glenn).

Buttons with State Seals or State Flowers ... pictures or both combined with button duplicates.

Buttons with Mementos of Foreign Travel ... There are many interesting angles to this classification. Foreign banknotes (most foreign paper money is of small denomination) are very handsome and colorful. Their designs are varied and easily duplicated in buttons. Combine a banknote, a coin, a button and a stamp from each foreign country and get a tremendously special collection. Don't forget ... buttons include "studs," gay, fancy, brightly colored souvenirs from ski areas, winter sports resorts, etc. (See Photograph No. 8.)

Buttons with Pressed Flowers ... surround a spray of pressed flowers with a ring of matching floral design buttons. Or make it with dried leaves, or heads of wheat and oats.

Buttons with Shells ... this, too, offers a wide field. Packages of mixed shells are cheap and the sort of souvenir one acquires without really trying. Match the shells to the buttons, or vice versa, and frame.

VERY, VERY SPECIAL: mount a wedding announcement and surround it with sample buttons from the bridal gown and trousseau and from the gowns of the wedding attendants. It will make a charming gift to the bride on her first wedding anniversary. The same idea can be worked for a baby shower, framing the invitation with a button from everyone attending the party. Special birthdays, (16th and 21st), school proms and engagement parties can all be memorialized this way.

A Suggested Shopping List

"Where do you find buttons worth collecting?" Any button is worth collecting if there is a real idea involved, such as in the little special collections we've just been talking about. Finding the buttons is no mystery.

Because buttons are important today from a fashion point of view, millions of them are being made and are for sale at the notions counters of department, variety, and dressmaking stores. When you see something you want, buy it right then and there! Despite the fact that buttons are manufactured by the millions, a particular style or size or shape may be sold out the next time you ask for it. This applies, of course, only to fancy buttons.

Fancy styles are short lived from the store manager's point of view. As soon as one line of fancies is sold out, he'll order a different line to keep his stock fresh and new and varied. Every now and then, to make room for new stock, he'll toss all kinds of styles and sizes into one bin and mark them all the same price to clear them out. This provides a wonderful chance to pick up unusual buttons at very little cost. Even if they don't fit your particular category, don't pass up the chance of buying some of the best ones. You can always use them for your clothes or trade them.

Church fairs and bazaars are sometimes a good source for finding unusual buttons. If the ladies running the booths are in the know, the chances of getting real button bargains are pretty slim, except for one thing. The majority of adults go after old and antique buttons. The young collector, concentrating on modern novelties, has a much wider field. Look over the displays carefully. You might find exactly what you're after in a dish of mixed up, apparently worthless buttons. Occasionally, you'll find a mason jar of underwear and shirt buttons on the White Elephant table. It probably came from someone who picked it up at a country auction because she thought it might be interesting, then changed her mind about the whole thing. If you can get it for fifteen or twenty-five cents, grab it. Someday you might want to make a modified

Costermonger's costume for a school play or party. Adults are beginning to collect underwear buttons and that jar might have some that you could trade.

Get on friendly terms with a couple of dry cleaners. They usually have large boxes of buttons that have come off garments. Naturally, the ones they consider valuable are not going to be in those boxes but everyone's sense of values, when it comes to collecting, is highly individual. Get permission to poke around and you might discover a few treasures.

Old-fashioned tailor shops—and there are still a lot of them—also frequently have varied collections of buttons. Permission to examine them is not difficult to obtain. If you find something you want, offer to pay for it. If the price is too high you can always pass it up. The chances are, however, that a token payment of five or ten cents will be mutually satisfactory. Tailor shops near military camps or naval bases are an excellent source of uniform buttons, as are tailor shops near railroad stations or yards and airports.

There are a few things to keep in mind about these transactions. Remember, business people are busy. Select a time for your visit that won't interfere with business. Wait until they are free before tackling them on your problem or desires. Tell the proprietor why you're looking for buttons. There's nothing like a good sound reason to secure his sympathy and co-operation.

You may run into some grumpy owners, but don't let that bother or discourage you. Thank them and go someplace else.

Keep your eye open for junk shops, antique and second-hand shops, thrift shops, Salvation Army stores, Women's Exchanges, and curio shops. While there may be nothing but lamps and furniture, old guns, chairs and china in the window, you might be pleasantly surprised at what the manager produces when you ask for buttons. Though many of these places do not deal in second-hand clothes, some get clothes with other purchases, cut off the buttons and keep them around.

Grandmothers and aunts usually have button boxes tucked away somewhere. Again, the specific approach will work wonders. "I'm looking for buttons for a school display." Or, "We're studying conservation and have to make posters. I thought you might have some buttons." Some older relatives might have been or still are button collectors themselves. If so, you're in. The older collector is usually happy to pass along to a young one the buttons she cannot use or has lost interest in. Older collectors are also usually eager to tell everything they know about buttons. Listen to them (a small price to pay for gifts) because there is plenty of information to be picked up in this field that has not yet been included in books on the subject.

And talking about books, your local librarian can be of great help. If the library does not own the book you're after, she can usually get it for you from another library or your state library. At the same time, the librarian can put you in touch with adult collectors in your area if you do not already know them. Some libraries, especially in rural and semirural districts, have display cases for exhibition purposes. Your own special collection combined with those of a few friends would make an interesting display if it is well organized and attractively presented. Talk it over with the librarian.

Farmer's Markets and country auctions are favorite haunts of button collectors of all ages. Watch experienced collectors operate at these sources. Notice how they examine and scrutinize the buttons or the collections that will go on sale. Watch them open every drawer, shake every box, pick up and turn mason jars of buttons to see if anything special will be revealed. They'll examine any old clothes, always looking for buttons. You, too, are privileged to do the same if and when the items are on exhibit before the sale begins. Once a sale has started the rule is hands off anything until you've bought it and it's yours.

Read the For Sale ads in small-town newspapers, hobby magazines, antiques journals and the National Button Society *Bulletin*. Button dealers offer all kinds of combinations as well as individual specimens. You can get assortments at a dollar and up. The buttons in these assortments are quite varied. What you can't use can be traded for ones you need. When any ad invites your inquiry, and many do, be sure to include a stamped, self-addressed envelope if you write to them, otherwise you'll get no answer.

One of the big manufacturers of buttons advertises a five-pound assortment of discontinued patterns. This includes a great variety, some of them scarce or rare. The price, about four dollars, may be high, depending upon your piggy bank. One of the ways you can reduce that price is to get several friends interested and split the cost. Another bonanza the manufacturers offer is a pound of shank buttons for two dollars, for use in making bracelets.

Among the discards from such bulk assortments will be plenty of items you can use on dresses, suits, sweaters and fashion accessories. There will be pairs for earrings and cuff links, a trim for your sneakers, and still quantities left over.

If you have friends or relatives living in other states or countries ask them to look around for buttons for you. It's a funny thing about buttons; they're all over the world waiting for a selective eye to see them, to choose them for a specific purpose. Your friend in California can pick up buttons that you can't possibly find in New Jersey. Californians get buttons from Mexico, Hawaii, Japan, Canada (Indian and Eskimo) that seldom reach the East Coast. Also, button manufacturers find that the Pacific Coast's taste and style of clothing are just enough different to require styles of buttons that wouldn't sell well in the East. So, renew your friendship with that California friend. Both of you may profit by it.

Look through the catalogs of Sears, Montgomery Ward and other mail order houses, especially the section showing dressmaking and sewing supplies. Check all women's magazines for advertisements from dressmaker supply houses. Check your local telephone book, particularly the classified pages. If a place sells sewing supplies, trimmings and notions, it's almost a sure thing that it will sell buttons as well.

Sort and mount your buttons on cards for sale at school, charity and church bazaars and Women's Exchanges. Convert some of your friends to the fun of button collecting by starting them off with a gift assortment. Use buttons to decorate birthday cards and notepaper. If your ingenuity gives out before the buttons do, store them away in a good strong box for the next generation to find and have fun with.

Be a Display Artist

The fun of collecting has many aspects. You can be content with simply amassing great numbers of an item and get a real kick out of counting and re-counting them. This is the form of gloating misers enjoy. The only important thing about it is the numbers involved. You may have 264 pin-backs but inevitably a boy on the next block, or across town, will have 302. That leaves you—where?

Naturally, anyone who collects is exerting a certain amount of selectivity. Out of all the millions of things in the world a young collector chooses one—pin-backs. If he carries his selectivity a step further and concentrates on nothing but red pin-backs, he's advanced a bit. But it still is no challenge to his intelligence, imagination and ingenuity. Those factors produce the real interest, fun and knowledge that collecting can give.

They are also necessary attributes when it comes to sharing your hobby with other people. This, of course, is the peak that all collectors reach sooner or later—a strong compulsion to communicate with others, to show off a little, to compare and get new ideas.

Adults get a tremendous kick out of entering trays of buttons in local, state and national shows, as well as displaying them at grange and church shows. The two-dollar or five-dollar prize means nothing as far as the money goes. But the honor of winning that modest prize is heart-warming and delightful. The congratulations you receive and the conversations it stimulates make you feel like a million. This is what keeps interest keyed up and study and ingenuity sharpened.

Junior collectors have a much wider range to play in than do adults. The number of ways button collections can be tailored to school uses alone is far greater than you might suppose. There is scarcely a subject in grade or high school that cannot be dramatized by displays of special button collections. The same old subjects assigned year after year have a wonderful way of perking up and becoming lively when given the button treatment. (See Photograph No. 14.)

Just think how you, with all your experience in

making posters and displays for school, church and grange, could go to town with button material! Handling it in a purely decorative and dramatic way, your interpretation and presentation of almost any assignment could be a show stopper. (See Photograph No. 7.)

The decorative side of displaying buttons and button collections has so many angles that ideas begin popping practically as soon as you start thinking about it.

It's easy enough to make an interesting pattern of buttons on a colored cardboard background. But the minute you frame such a pattern you add importance and significance to the display.

Frames are easy and cheap to come by. Practically every household has a few frames not in use. Or pick up one in a junk shop (you won't need the glass), clean it up or paint it as its condition requires. Or, if you've been having paper folding and sculpture in school, you know all about making frames from bristol or cardboard. Here's the chance to put that knowledge to use.

Having settled on the frame, cut a piece of heavy cardboard to fit into it. This must be fairly sturdy since the material you are going to mount has some weight. Choose a color that goes with the display material and the idea involved. Clear, brilliant colors are fine for military or uniform buttons. The more feminine type of button calls for more delicate and subtle colors. The one thing to remember is never let the color of the background dominate the display. It should throw it into relief and dramatize it. Lay the buttons and their companion display on the background and arrange them first this way and then that until you are satisfied with the pattern achieved.

Once the pattern has been determined, lightly mark the background to indicate the exact position of each item. Check these marks with a ruler, for these displays call for mathematical precision.

There are several ways of mounting buttons so that they'll stay in place for the life of the display. When buttons have shanks, make a small slit in the background, thrust the shank through and anchor it on the back with a short length of pipestem cleaner. If the buttons are sew-throughs, do just that. Only a single stitch of heavy thread is required through each hole. Knot the thread tightly on the back of the display. Or, you can mount cach button with rubber cement. This allows you to remove the buttons later; the cement can be rubbed off the button without harming it.

Once the material is mounted, fit it into the frame and back it up with the first piece of heavy cardboard you cut to size. Small wire brads are then pushed into the inside edge of the frame to hold the display; that is, if the frame is of wood. Otherwise, seal the display into the frame with masking tape.

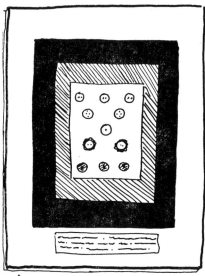
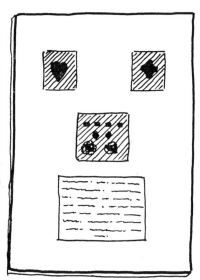

Mounting Buttons for Display.

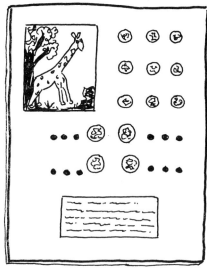

Thin plywood makes a good base. Use rubber cement for mounting materials so they can be removed for re-use. Typed explanations are major part of display. Experiment with arrangements and colors.

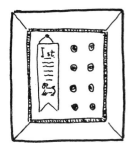  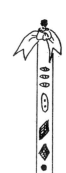

Framing Special Collections.

Inexpensive dime store frames offer wide range for small special collections. Cover backing with fabric or colored paper before mounting buttons and allied subjects. Discard glass; it won't fit. Hang in groups of three or more to give importance and dramatic effect.

Use odd buttons on tired accessories. They're fun to make, use.

Fun Fashions.

Five and ten cent stores and some supermarkets have inexpensive metal frames that can be used quite effectively for small button displays. Ranging in price from fourteen to thirty-nine cents, they give a professional finish to a small display that is very acceptable. These metal frames are cut in one piece and secured at the bottom with a small flange. Bend this flange back just enough to open the frame. Remove glass, picture and cardboard, using the latter as a base for mounting your display. This can be covered with satin or velvet or construction paper and the buttons mounted directly on it. Save the glass. It won't fit into the frame with your material but you may want to use it later for something else.

Suppose you have only four buttons having some special significance. Four, you think, are certainly not enough for a display. But they are if you do it this way. Frame each one separately, centering it in a small velvet-backed metal frame. Then frame all four in a much larger frame whose background color will dramatize the four small frames. This same trick can be interpreted in a different way. Simply mount each button on a square of colored paper and then mount the paper against a main larger background.

Descriptive matter usually is required. Hand-letter the text if you can or type it and mount it on a card to be shown beside your framed exhibit. When the show is over it can be pasted on the back of the display for identification and description. Be sure it is dated and has your name on it.

Have you ever heard of or seen a button garden? It is an enchanting thing, easily made and serves as a delightful gift or favor. Real buttons and real plants are used, and the gardens actually live and grow! (See Photograph No. 6.)

Large plain buttons with flat backs, the kind used on men's overcoats, or larger if you can get them, serve as "flower pots" and tiny seedlings of cacti and succulents are the plants. Mrs. Florence Casebolt of California dreamed up this idea. She wrote an interesting book about it. Perhaps your library can get it for you if none of the button collectors in your area have it. It is called *Button Gardens and Flower Arrangements* and is well worth reading.

The root systems of minute plants are extremely small and pliable which makes it possible to use them in this way. Spread a very thin layer of sandy soil in the depression of the button. Set the seedling on it, spreading the roots so they will help balance the plant and keep it upright. Sometimes it might be necessary to use a tiny pebble or two to prop up the plant. Cover the roots, lightly, with more sandy soil. It is possible to use two or three plants on the same button. The addition of minute figures, the kind you get in Japanese stores, adds interest and increases the illusion.

You can, of course, go out and buy tiny cacti and succulents for this purpose but it's easier and cheaper to beg them from window gardeners or to raise them yourself. Or, for volume production, one fifty-cent packet of seeds will provide you with more plants than you can get any other way.

These button gardens are so fascinating to create that you will probably make dozens of them. But what will you do with them?

They make charming gifts for older people—grand-mothers, aunts and friends of your mother. Best of all, they make excellent gifts for people in hospitals or invalids at home.

A group of girls and two boys recently made quite a number of button gardens and donated them to their local hospital. Nurses loved them because they are so tiny they require practically no space. The only care they need is watering with an eye dropper, a few drops when the soil looks dry. Patients love them because the variety of textures and colors possible in these tiny gardens make them constantly interesting. People in hospitals often become bored with stiff bouquets and large potted plants, but a button garden, so easy to take care of, is always welcome.

A gift of the "makings" to a convalescent child will provide unusual entertainment that will keep him amused and interested without taxing his strength. Put several large flat buttons in a box along with some tiny weeds or a few seedling plants. Add colored pebbles and tiny shells or anything else that is extremely small and appropriate for a garden design. A lump of modeling clay will complete the outfit. Later, when he is out of bed, he can rearrange his garden using sandy soil for planting.

Another type of button garden is the kind you can hang on the wall! Dump out that mason jar or your box of discards and select as many different size pearl buttons as you can. Think of a prim, old-fashioned garden where the plants are lined up in stiff rows. The pearl buttons will be the flower heads and you'll paint in the stems and leaves with poster paint. Don't try to be accurate or realistic. Do it quickly with strokes that are like kindergarten drawings. Use Sobo adhesive for pasting on buttons and rickrack. Paste a line or two of rickrack across the bottom, and there's a delightful button garden! The one illustrated (Photograph No. 1) is done on dark brown construction paper with white stems and leaves. The top row of rickrack is dark green, the other two, white. The frame is a pair of embroidery hoops.

Another way of framing this kind of button picture is to mount the design on a small cocktail tray or an aluminum pie plate or even a paper plate. The paper and aluminum plates, dishes and containers designed for freezing foods offer a wealth of background possibilities. Even their covers can serve as mounts for small arrangements.

The number of ways you can use buttons to decorate paper items is legion. Party place cards; Christmas, anniversary and birthday cards; even notepaper and invitations can be amusingly decorated with simple designs worked out with buttons. Sobo adhesive is strong and lasting and will withstand the ravages of a trip through the post office. Amusing stick figures can be drawn and buttons used for the heads, wheels on toy trains, wagons, roller skates, etc. Flower sprays become more decorative when one or two small buttons are used for the flower heads. Turn on your imagination.

Most of the things a girl wears offers possibilities for being enhanced by buttons. Combs, clips, hairpins, necklaces, bracelets, belts, earrings, cuff links and bobby pins are some of the items that can be decorated with buttons. Pocket flaps, yokes, collars, headbands, sweaters, mittens and gloves, sports socks and sneakers, all offer splendid opportunities for designing with buttons.

Admittedly, there's a limit to the amount of button-trimmed fashions you might want to have and wear. But many of these button-trimmed items offer fringe benefits that perhaps you hadn't thought of. Small towns and rural communities are always giving bazaars and fairs for one worthy cause or another. Almost anything will sell at them if it is cleverly designed, well made, unusual and modestly priced. Decide which button-trimmed items you and your friends want to make.

As well as fashion accessories, children's toys, bookmarks, button gardens, small button pictures, birthday and greeting cards all have sales appeal. Make up a few perfect samples and show them to an adult who has had some experience in selling at church bazaars and sales. She may have suggestions for improvements or simplifications that will make the items more saleable. Don't let your feelings get hurt if she gives you no encouragement. She could be wrong. Consult someone else. The first person may be so interested in tatting or pickling that she can't see anything outside of those two endeavors. If two out of three adults approve of your ideas and think they're saleable, go ahead. You can't lose.

How to Make Beautiful Buttons

D espite the thousands of styles of buttons that are available all over the country, there are times when finding exactly what you want for a specific dress or suit seems impossible. Then make them!

One can create individual and quite handsome buttons in many ways. Of course, the most obvious of all, covering the button shapes you buy, is child's play and rather unimaginative. For certain styles, however, it is perhaps the best way. But, today is the day of the large, dramatic, beautiful button—the button that has individuality as well as looks. It is the time to exploit some of the skills you've learned in school or picked up in leisure hours.

Many junior and senior high schools give pottery

and ceramic courses. If your school doesn't, the chances are good that an adult education program in your area offers such courses. It might pay you to consider the possibilities.

Making pottery or ceramic buttons is quite simple. It can be done at home but the facilities provided by schools and workshops make production simpler. They have kilns for firing as well as a larger selection of glazes to work with than does a home hobby outfit.

Buttons can be any shape—round, square, oblong, diamond, oval or realistic (the shape of a pear or a banana, for instance). The trick to making ceramic buttons is thickness (not less than ⅜″ because they shrink in drying) and having a perfectly flat back. Size is optional, depending upon how spectacular you want them to be. The most successful and easiest arrangement for attaching ceramic buttons is two or more holes for sewing them on. The holes are pierced *after* the design has either been pressed or carved on. Small butter or German cookie molds work wonderfully well. Wet the mold and simply press it on a clay pat. Trim away outer edge either realistically if design allows or in the desired shape. Let the clay button dry thoroughly; then follow the procedure for glazing, as instructed by your pottery teacher, or as given in your how-to manual.

The Cooper Union Museum of the Arts of Decoration, in New York City, has in its comprehensive collection of rare, antique, historic and modern buttons a number of simple pottery buttons that are quite charming. They are square and bear a small decorative modern design. The thing that is most interesting about them is that they illustrate a number of different ways of handling the colored glazes. One button is entirely glazed, top and edges, in a single color. Another uses one color for the design, and a different color for the background. Still another allows the design to retain its original terra cotta color while the background is glazed. The next one reverses this method—glazing the design and letting the background stay as is. These variations on a theme are an interesting presentation of the variety possible within the confines of one single simple design.

Some clays do not require the high firing heat provided by kilns. Hobby stores and art shops stock various clays that can be baked in the kitchen oven. They will not produce as permanent a button as the traditional pottery type of clay but, on the other hand, for experimenting and limited wear, they will work out pretty well. After baking, this type of clay is colored with poster paints and then varnished.

Copper wire, an unusual material for making buttons, can be used alone or combined with wooden but-

9. Pin-Backs

A card of rare pin-backs. Untold billions have
been manufactured since their first appearance
in 1896 for the McKinley presidential campaign.

10. A Pearly Queen Costume

A modern Pearly Queen costume, decorated with thousands of pearl buttons, is
the London Costermonger's festive outfit.

Courtesy of Mrs. Marion Lawson

11. Trolley Cars, Fraternals, Defense

Popular with men and boys are buttons from uniforms, military and civil. Shown are examples from trolley car companies, fraternal clubs, and defense outfits.

Courtesy of Harold Van Buren

12. Buttons of the 19th Century

Preserved are those from grandmother's going-away outfit, mounted with an old-fashioned print of the period.

13. Fancy Buttons

Fancy buttons, from the extensive collection
at the Cooper Union Museum in New York City.

Courtesy of Cooper Union Museum

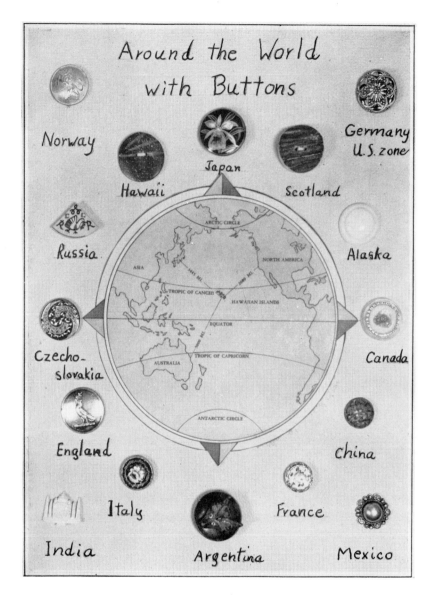

14. *Around the World with Buttons*

A prize-winning display, recently shown at a National Button Society Show, offers ideas for similar school displays.

15. Buttons in 18th Century Costume

Fine workmanship, rich materials and lovely designs are characteristic of 18th century buttons. These are from the Cooper Union Museum in New York City.

Courtesy of Cooper Union Museum

16. Sporting Buttons

Old and new sporting buttons. The spoked automobile
wheel is a modern Dorset button. Ski resort buttons
are made of paper discs mounted on plastic button bases.

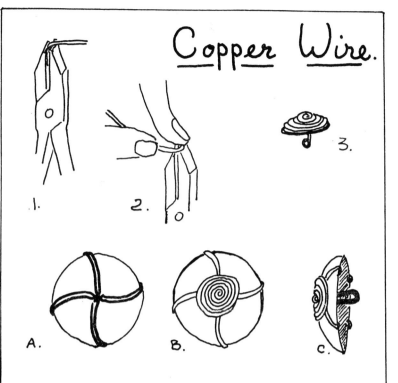

Copper Wire.

1.

2.

3.

A.

B.

C.

A 12" length of copper wire (18 gauge) will be enough for a ¾" button. One inch from end make a right-angled bend and hold in the pliers as shown in sketch #1. Swing long end clockwise at top of pliers, sketch #2, while turning the pliers counter-clockwise. Coils must touch each other. After three or four turns, rest of coiling is easier done without the pliers. When flat coil is desired size, turn wire under outer edge of coil and cut off surplus, if any. The short vertical piece in the center is shank of button, sketch #3. Turn its end up to make a loop for sewing on. A, B, C show wire decoration on a wooden button mold having a single center hole. Spokes are laid separately, their ends bent under edge of mold. Flat coil is made. Shank slips through center hole. Bend double to hold coil in place.

ton molds and beads. The best weight to work with is 14 gauge. Photograph No. 2 shows a pair of coiled wire buttons using the technique invented by the ancient Egyptians. They used gold wire, and examples of the jewelry they made with coiled gold wire may be seen in the Metropolitan Museum of Art in New York City.

The only tools required for coiling copper wire are your fingers and jewelers' pliers for cutting. A tiny loop is bent in the end of the wire (this is the shank for sewing button to garment); then, ⅜″ above the loop the wire is bent at a right angle and coiled around to the desired size. The shank and ⅜″ long shaft is held by the pliers in the right hand while the thumb and fingers of the left eases the wire around and around. The first time you do this the operation will seem awkward and balky. Expect to waste a few inches of wire until you get the knack, which will come suddenly. When the coiled wire disk is the size you want, cut it off and use the pliers to bend the cut end in and under the disk.

Variations on this theme, combined with wooden molds and beads, make extremely effective buttons for tweeds and woolen jackets and suits. To keep the copper wire from tarnishing, coat it with two thin applications of colorless nail polish.

One of the simplest and easiest ways of individualizing buttons is to decorate an otherwise plain plastic button with paper cutouts. Magazines are filled with illustrations that can be used this way. In the lower picture, Photograph No. 16, the buttons that look like souvenirs of such famous ski resorts as Stowe, Sun Valley, Aspen and Sugarloaf are 1½″ plastic buttons with raised rims. The designs are from an advertisement, cut to fit the buttons' inside diameter. Before pasting in the paper designs, two strands (one through each pair of holes) of embroidery floss, long enough to use for sewing the button on with, are threaded through the holes and tied together tightly at the back. Paste the paper circle to the face of the button, making sure that it fits exactly and adheres completely at every point. When dry, the paper circles may be coated with varnish or colorless nail polish to preserve them.

Any number of small motifs may be used—flowers, bugs, drawings, portraits, abstract designs, slogans, even ones you make up yourself. The variety is limitless, as even the most brief run-through of any magazine will prove. Caution: use only rimmed buttons. The rim protects the applied design when the button is slipped in and out of the buttonhole.

Metal button forms on sale in notions departments can be decorated in other ways than the usual one of covering them with material. Try painting them. Poster paint, household enamel, artist's oil paint—all may be used. With any of these paints, however, the surface of the button mold must be prepared. Sandpaper or steel wool the entire surface to provide sufficient roughness for the paint to catch on and hold. After sandpapering, wash the surface with soap and water and rinse very thoroughly. From this point on never touch the surface with your fingers! There is sufficient oil in your skin to adhere to metal and affect the paint.

These metal form buttons all have shanks for sewing on. Hold the button shank in a spring type clothespin while painting and decorating. Leave the clothespin on the shank to support the wet button in a juice or other small glass until the paint is dry. When dry, protect it with varnish or nail polish. The smallest can of McCloskey's Heirloom varnish will do dozens of buttons and give a far more satisfactory protective coat than nail polish.

With the great variety of embroidered ribbons now available, one has an equally great variety of possibilities for individual, custom made buttons. Centering a single strip of embroidered ribbon over the dress fabric used to cover the button is most attractive. Baste it to the circle of cloth before covering the button. This will keep it in position while snapping the back into place. Several strips of embroidered ribbon may be sewn together to cover the button entirely—a good trick to know when the same ribbon is used to bind or trim other parts of the garment. (See top two buttons, Photograph No. 5.)

The roll-up button is one of the oldest forms of homemade button, dating back to the sixteenth century. (See Photograph No. 4.) It is nothing more than a long, triangular piece of cloth, rolled up on itself and sewn into position. The one illustrated is about the size and shape of a small egg. The wool fabric was cut in a triangle 2″ wide at the bottom tapering to a point 12″ above the bottom. The sides were cut with pinking shears, which not only prevent the fabric from raveling but give a decorative sawtooth edge. A little experimenting is necessary since the thickness of the fabric determines the thickness of the button. With thin fabrics a much longer triangle is necessary to achieve a button of any substantial character. Thin fabrics can be backed with pellon or similar interfacing before rolling up. With the press-on type of interfacing, cut the triangle wide enough to allow for turning in the edges. These buttons are, for the most part, purely decorative although they can be functional when used with loops rather than buttonholes.

Cord, alone or covered with velvet, may be woven into most attractive decorative buttons. A form of sailor's knotting, the flat weave button is worked from

FLAT WEAVE BUTTON: Lay loops 1, 2, 3, 4 as shown being careful to go over and under in sequence. Outside loops determine finished size of button. Continue weaving *inside* original loops until all spaces are solidly packed. Number of times required depends upon size of cord used. Sew outside edges to cloth-covered form.

CHINESE BUTTON: Lay loops 1, 2, 3 as shown. Hold ends in hand and work loops down tight, one at a time. The size of button depends upon size of cord used. Leave short ends to sew on.

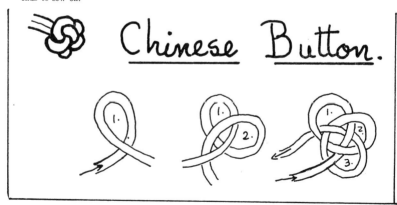

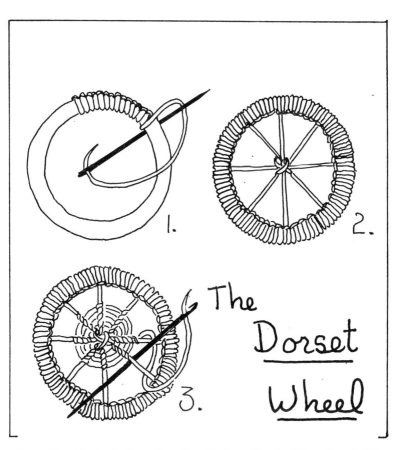

1. 2. 3.

The Dorset Wheel

Use a café curtain ring for frame. Cover ring with close buttonhole stitch as shown in #1; using heavy pearl embroidery thread or sport yarn. When ring is covered, do not break off thread. Slide stitches around so buttonhole edging lies inside ring. Lay spokes across ring, spacing them evenly, with unused length of thread. Secure them at center with two cross stitches as shown in #2. Spokes must be taut and firmly tied. With same thread, backstitch over each spoke, as shown in #3. Threads between spokes should lie evenly and close together. Continue around and around until wheel is filled. To finish, run thread up to center through back of one spoke and use to sew button to garment. If two or more colors are desired, be sure that each band of color is completed before starting another color. This same technique may be used to cover a convex button mold having a center hole. Lay spokes and weave.

the outside edge into the center. When the loops are drawn up tightly, the popular Chinese soft button is formed. When worked flat, as was the velvet rope button in the photograph, a large and dramatic button is achieved. Done this way the button must be mounted on a stiff backing, both for attaching it to the garment and for preserving the design.

One way to do this is to cover a large metal button form with matching color fabric to which the woven knot button is then slip-stitched around the edges. Or, cut a cardboard shape to match the outside edge of the button, cover it, and sew on.

The roll-up button, if securely sewn, can be laundered or dry-cleaned. The flat weave, when worked in silk or velvet-covered cord, can be dry-cleaned if it is mounted on a regular button mold or form. Whether cardboard would stand up under dry cleaning is doubtful. However, this kind of decorative button can be removed before the garment is sent to the cleaners. If the button has become soiled, you might find it easy to swish it around in a cleaning fluid yourself rather than risk its being mangled or squashed by the dry cleaners.

Needlework is a phrase that covers embroidery, crocheting, making hairpin lace and needle weaving. The latter is a technique used by the old Dorset Button makers and goes as far back as the fifteenth century.

In the old days, a small wad of wool or cotton or cloth was decoratively covered with various weaving stitches. This required an extremely slow and painstaking technique, hardly practicable today. The simplest form of needle weaving, that can be rather quickly done, is the method illustrated on page 73. A café curtain ring is covered with the buttonhole stitch. Then spokes are laid across the ring at even distances and tied together at the center. The thread is then woven around these spokes to fill in the center of the ring.

Another good way of needle weaving is to work on a button mold having a center hole. The spokes are laid across and through the hole, tied securely, and then serve as a base for needle weaving around them. Both of these buttons can be worked up rather quickly (after a little practice) and can be laundered or dry-cleaned with no danger.

The possibilities for embroidering buttons, one of the handsomest ways of decoration, are limited only by your skill, imagination and patience. The button molds you buy at notions counters are supplied with cutout guides for fabric covering. Use the guide to draw a circle on your fabric but don't cut it out until after the embroidery is completed. You can work freehand in an allover design or center various motifs as you desire. The embroidered button illustrated (Photo-

Designs for Painting
and Embroidering Buttons.

graph No. 5) uses small scale cross-stitch, a most effective way of working out a geometrical design.

Embroidery design actually determines the kind of embroidery stitches you'll use. Since the designs are necessarily small, the stitches must be equally so. The work is best done in embroidery hoops and can be as elaborate or as simple as desired. Nothing could be smarter for summer clothes than hand-embroidered buttons. (See rooster, Photograph No. 5.) Cotton threads are color fast, so laundering offers no problems. Tapestry wools used for petit point embroideries are wonderfully apt for embroidering buttons for sweaters and cardigans; or, for that matter, garments that will be dry-cleaned rather than laundered. They cover the surface quickly and come in magnificent subtle colors.

For a very special evening jacket or sweater, petit point buttons offer a rich and beautiful accent. Use the cutting guide from the button mold package to draw the outside dimension right on the petit point canvas. One quarter of an inch inside that circle draw another circle. The petit point embroidery ends at this circle.

A length of narrow hairpin lace, made with a gold or silver metallic thread, can be joined to make a circle and mounted on a fabric covered button. This is a quite rapid method of making an effective decoration. The outside loops of the lace are securely slip-stitched to the fabric cover of the button. Naturally, the size of the button controls the width of the lace. Hairpin lace frames, from extremely narrow to quite wide, may be bought at notions counters. A three-quarter inch frame was used for the gold cord daisy button in Photograph No. 5, lower right-hand corner.

When Irish crochet lace was popular (and it shows signs of coming back), crocheted buttons were the only kind used. They varied from ¼″ on up, depending upon the design of the garment. Worked with the finest thread, they were extremely dainty. Today's crocheted buttons start at ¾″ and go up, and are usually made of fine knitting wool. Single crochet stitch is the commonest form, using a 3-chain circle to start with. But you can use other stitches—bullion, petal, popcorn. Any crochet instruction book will supply the know-how of these basic stitches. The main point to remember is to keep the work firm and close so that the button mold is entirely concealed. If a particular stitch you want to use allows the background to show through, either feature that point by covering the mold with a definitely contrasting color or cover the mold with a matching color. (See Photograph No. 3.)

Beautifully made buttons can be created by anyone willing to spend a little time in practicing and experimenting. As in any other art or skill, the first few productions will probably be unsatisfactory, even a little crude. Remember the first few times you set your hair on rollers? The results were pretty sad! All of a sudden, though, the right technique seemed to flow from your fingers. Now you can do it like a pro. The same thing applies here. A bit of practice is needed, practice that will produce speed and perfection.

Handsome handmade buttons, when mounted on cards, can be sold at bazaars and community charity sales. It might be well, in this case, to stick with conventional and popular colors. You may indicate that special orders can be taken for off-beat shades or unusual combinations. This is an excellent way for young people to contribute to local enterprises. They can share their proceeds or donate the buttons outright. With the tremendous popularity that the decorative button enjoys today, a ready-made market might emerge in your own community, over and above your co-operation with sales and bazaars.

Many other ways of making buttons will probably occur to you once you start fiddling around with ideas and materials. Try them. You can't lose and you may arrive at something extremely individual and good looking. Any creative effort is valuable. Who can tell? Perhaps a hundred years from now your handmade buttons will be just as precious and sought after by collectors as are the embroidered, painted and pottery buttons of a hundred years ago.

A Button Time Table

The most civilized peoples of early times, the Greeks and the Romans, used *fibulae* (pins) to hold garments together. Thousands of fibulae have been found by archaeologists. The earliest ones looked like this:

VI–V B.C.

Wire, one end of which was sharpened and the other flattened, was coiled at the center to provide spring and to bring the ends together. Many later fibulae were decorated with elaborate designs that were attached to the top part. Made of beaten or hammered gold, these decorations were very handsome.

III B.C.

The first real buttons (see Chapter 2) were excavated from a Danish peat bog. They had holes in them for sewing or permanently attaching them to garments. With the present interest and activity in archaeological research, it is quite possible that new excavations will uncover real buttons dating much further back in time than do the Danish ones.

VI–VII A.D.

This drawing certainly looks like a button but it isn't. It's a rosette-shaped fibula showing great skill and artistry in its design of colored stones and delicate coilings of gold wire surrounding the stones. In today's button language it would be called a "pin-back." Hundreds of these rosette-shaped fibulae have been found. Their shape made people think that they actually were buttons. This one is "Frankish." The Franks were a Teutonic Eastern Barbarian race who invaded Germany and northern France.

XII–XIII A.D.

The illustrations of ancient manuscripts and missals (prayer books) show that buttons were used to close the diagonal neckline of men's garments. Women used lacing to close and make their garments fit snugly. As clothes became even more fitted, long rows of buttons were used on both male and female dress, particularly along the outside seam of sleeves, from wrist to shoulder. This style cropped up for hundreds of years. During this period, the two basic shapes of buttons, the small ball button and the flat round one, appeared. They were used both functionally and decoratively and were set so close together that they touched each other.

During the next four centuries, the decorative quality of buttons was emphasized. Buttons grew in size up to three inches in diameter or shrank to less than one-quarter of an inch, as fashion dictated. All the arts and skills of jewelers and tailors were employed to make buttons things of beauty. Many different kinds of materials were used as well as varied techniques.

Metal buttons were decorated with designs cut into the surface (chasing); or had designs hammered into the back so that the fronts showed in raised patterns (*repoussé*); or were elaborately set with precious, semi-precious or just colored stones. Fine gold or silver wires were coiled and twisted into lacy patterns and soldered to the surface of buttons.

Cloth-covered buttons were embellished with fine and delicate embroidery. Ivory, stones and shells were carved into buttons of various sizes. Silk or metal cords were coiled and woven into intricate patterns that covered the button mold. Enameling (powdered glass in wonderful colors fired at high heat to melt and harden) on copper was another technique used to produce exquisite buttons.

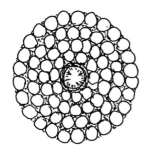

XVI A.D.

During the Elizabethan period (1558–1605 A.D.), extremely elaborate jewelry and fantastically fancy clothing somewhat overshadowed the importance of buttons in court circles. But they did not disappear from the scene entirely. Ordinary people used them in great quantities, ranging from simple cloth and metal ones to quite rich and valuable ones. Sir Walter Raleigh had himself painted in a magnificent costume of white and gold, down the front of which were seventeen buttons, each an inch and a half in diameter. One large real pearl was set in the center of each button and was surrounded by a solid paving of small pearls. The Duke of Buckingham, a famous dandy of the time, went Raleigh one better by having his buttons set with real diamonds.

Watches, cased in magnificent examples of the jeweler's art, had become very popular. By 1622, they were being made small enough to be worn as earrings and finger rings. Cardinal Richelieu of France wore a series of three-quarter-inch watches as buttons!

XVII A.D.

By this time it was no longer possible to tell the social status of people by the buttons they wore. Oxford University attempted to solve the problem with a set of rules that its scholars were supposed to follow. On August 27, 1666, the Oxford rules, printed in English, so the tailors could read them, and in Latin for the benefit of the scholars, were posted. In simple language they said:

Servants [many students brought their personal servants with them] were to wear no buttons at all.

The commoner's gown was to have a half dozen buttons on each sleeve, not to cost more than five shillings the dozen and not to be larger than "the bigness of the public patternes."

A gentleman commoner could wear four dozen buttons on each gown, same price and size as above.

A baronet and a knight could also wear four dozen buttons on each gown but, if they wished, these could be of gold or silver. (A baronet was a hereditary title, passing from father to oldest son. A knight was an honorary title that went out of existence when the person bearing it died.)

It was during the seventeenth century that men really latched on to buttons and used them in vast quantities. Towards the end of this century their size, too, increased.

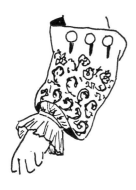

XVIII A.D.

The richness of the buttons used on men's costumes during most of the eighteenth century (see Photograph No. 15) was equalled only by the elaborately embroidered buttonholes and the decorative embroidery used on their waistcoats and coats. Tailors were prepared to supply the following kinds of buttons: thread, metal and worsted, death's head buttons, and ones made of mohair; gold and silver wire buttons, as well as shell, carnelian and tortoise-shell buttons; marcasite and cut steel, lapis lazuli and coin, knit, horsehair and pewter buttons; French gilt and London plate, embroidered, jeweled and bullion buttons and, of course, cloth-covered ones.

Buttons had disappeared from women's costumes and were not to become important again to female dress until after the middle of the nineteenth century. Following the American and French revolutions, both the size and number of buttons worn by men decreased, and buttons became much plainer in appearance. Usually of metal, brass or silver plate, they were used decoratively rather than functionally.

XIX A.D.

In England, at the beginning of this century, it became quite fashionable for young men to drive coaches. This new sport gave rise to various clubs— "The Whip Club," "Barouche Club," "Tandem Club," etc. In 1809, the Four-in-Hand Club had special buttons engraved for its members. This was the beginning of the vast number of men's clubs that used buttons for identification, a custom which still exists. Button collectors call this type "fraternals." (See Photograph No. 11 and upper No. 16.)

Towards the middle of the nineteenth century, buttons began to disappear from men's clothes and re-appear on women's costumes. The first buttoned boots (shoes) were marketed in 1860, first for men and then for women and children. From then on until World War I, laced shoes were reserved for utilitarian purposes and the working classes. So general and generous was the use of buttons by women from the 1850's on, that many thousands of them still exist. (See Photograph No. 12.) By 1870, the popularity of the Charm String was sufficiently widespread to inspire a popular song, "Give My Button String to Sister." The words were written by Florence Linley, and

the music by Charlie L. Ward. It was sadly sentimental
and the first verse went like this:

> "Give my button string to Sister,
>   I'll not want it any more.
> E're the morrow sun is shining
>   I'll be on the Golden Shore.
> Tell my sister when she's older,
>   When she first begins to sing,
> That her angel sister left her,
>   All her pretty button string."

XX A.D.

Buttons took a nosedive during and after World War I.
They did not regain their popularity until the 1940's. From
then until today, buttons have
been moving forward in leaps
and bounds. Their manufacture exceeds several billions a
year. The use of expensive materials—diamonds, pearls,
precious stones, etc.—which disappeared at the turn of
the nineteenth century will probably never come back.
However, the use of fancy buttons by men is once again
creeping into fashion. Decoratively designed metal buttons
now appear on men's and boys' sport jackets. Recently, a
New York jeweler ran a series of advertisements offering
14k. gold buttons for men's jackets. This is a trend worth
watching.

Goofies, Pin-backs, and Others

The scope of design and materials for buttons is enormous. Interestingly enough, modern buttons, with all the technological and manufacturing know-how involved, have not surpassed the old and the antique designs except in one respect—they are frequently object-shaped. The National Button Society calls them "realistic" or "goofies." The old ones, for instance, placed the picture of a monkey on a conventional shaped button face. Today's monkey button is the actual shape of a monkey. These object-shaped buttons make up a very large classification in button shows and competitions.

Run your eye over the list below. It will give you an idea of what the scope of goofies is. It will also help you make a logical and recognizable classification of the buttons you have already acquired, and may help you identify some puzzling goofies:

accessories	children	men
(*hats, lipsticks,*	cupids	musical
shoes, etc.)	(*also dwarfs,*	instruments
amphibians	*fairies,*	musicians
anchors	*mermaids*)	nuts
animals	fish	orientals
baskets	flowers	sports
birds	foods	sports equip-
boats	fruits	ment
bows	insects	transportation
buildings	leaves	women
candy	mammals	

Pin-backs, (see Photograph No. 9), collected at one time or another by practically every American boy, are tremendously interesting to adults as well as young people. Their real name is "celluloid lapel button," and they were patented by Whitehead & Hoag of Newark, New Jersey, in 1894.

The presidential campaign of 1896 launched pin-backs. Mark Hanna, campaign manager of the Republican nominee, William McKinley, placed an initial order for 5,000,000 pin-backs bearing McKinley's photo. The Democrats immediately followed suit and flooded the country with pin-backs of their nominee, William Jennings Bryan.

The Wendell Willkie campaign used more than 54,000,000, and a good deal more than 75,000,000 pin-backs helped elect Dwight D. Eisenhower. Between political campaigns, all kinds of things and events served to produce more pin-backs. At the turn of this century, Sweet Caporal cigarettes used pin-backs as premiums, a different one on every package. To keep interest active and to increase sales, many pictorial series were devised. Sets of State Seals, Flags, Actresses, Warships, Monarchs, Animals, Pugilists, Jockeys kept boys needling their fathers to buy specific brands. A famous newspaper comic character, the Yellow Kid, appeared in over three hundred different poses on pin-backs. So did the Katzenjammer Kids and other popular funny paper personalities.

Naturally, these older pin-backs are very desirable from the collector's point of view. However, despite the millions that were issued there are not too many around. The reason for their scarcity is that as interest in them waned they were tossed in the trash can and destroyed. This is normal procedure, particularly when they were obtained for free or at minimum cost.

What was true yesterday, in this respect, is just as true today. The pin-backs you've picked up in the last year will probably disappear via the Department of

Sanitation. However, a little selectivity and fore-thought on your part can turn them into a minor bank account twenty-five years from now. For instance: the 1953 Eisenhower Inauguration button that sold for ten cents brought a dollar at the Spring Antique Show in New York in April of 1962. John F. Kennedy and John Glenn pin-backs are going to be worth quite a bit if they (the pin-backs) survive for twenty-five years.

The possibility of modern buttons achieving antique status is quite likely for a number of reasons. If they are pretty or unusual, their chances of being saved are very high simply because more people are aware of and know more about buttons today. Then, the thrift instinct, still strong in a majority of women and girls, will prevent the destruction of many buttons. Also, young people using buttons in school and club work, for interior decoration and gifts, for money raising activities, and as special mementos and souvenirs are apt to see to it that their creative efforts and ingenuity will not be tossed out willy-nilly.

Playing with buttons, collecting buttons, using buttons creatively can produce rich rewards in new friendships, interest, enjoyment and the exploration of fresh fields of knowledge. Try it.

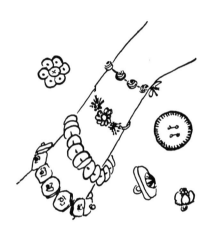

BIBLIOGRAPHY

ALBERT, ALPHAEUS H.: *Washington Historical Buttons,* Hightstown, N. J., 1949.

ALBERT, LILLIAN SMITH: The Complete Button Book, Hightstown, N. J., 1949.

————: *A Button Collector's Journal,* Hightstown, N. J., 1941.

————: *A Button Collector's Second Journal,* Hightstown, N. J., 1943.

————, and Adams, Jane Ford: *The Button Sampler,* M. Barrows & Co., Inc., New York, 1951.

CASEBOLT, FLORENCE: *Button Gardens & Diminutive Arrangements,* Button Garden Studio, Berkeley, Calif., 1952.

COUSE, ERWINNA, and MAPLE, MARGARET: *Button Classics,* Lightner Press, Chicago, 1941.

CRUMMOTT, POLLY DE S.: *Button Collecting,* Lightner Press, Chicago, 1939.

DAVENPORT, MILLIA: *The Book of Costume,* Vols. 1 and 2, Crown Publishers, Inc., New York, 1948.

DE WITT, J. DOYLE: *A Century of Campaign Buttons,* Travelers Press, Hartford, Conn., 1959.

EARLE, ALICE MORSE: *Two Centuries of Costume in America,* The Macmillan Co., New York, 1903.

EMILIO, LUIS FENOLOSSA: *The Emilio Collection,* Essex Institute, Salem, Mass., 1911.

FORD, GRACE HORNEY: *The Button Collector's History,* Pond-Ekberg, Springfield, Ill., 1943.

JOHNSON, DAVID F.: *American Historical Buttons,* Century House, Watkins Glen, N. Y., 1942.

———: *Uniform Buttons, American Armed Forces,* Century House, Watkins Glen, N. Y., 1948.

LESTER, KATHERINE: *Accessories of Dress,* Manual Arts Press, Peoria, Ill., 1940.

NICHOLLS, FRANCIS E.: *Button Handbook,* Cayuga Press, Ithaca, N. Y., 1943.

SHULL, THELMA: *The Button String,* Lightner Press, Chicago, 1942.

MAGAZINES

Antiques Journal, Uniontown, Penna., has a regular monthly button column.

Hobbies, The Magazine for Collectors, Chicago, Ill., a monthly magazine, frequently publishes articles on buttons.

Just Buttons, Southington, Conn., a monthly magazine.

National Button Bulletin, a quarterly issued by the National Button Society, c/o Mrs. Lillian Smith Albert, 353 Stockton St., Hightstown, N. J.

Spinning Wheel, Taneytown, Md., a monthly magazine with frequent button articles.

Index

abacus, 15
accessories, fashion, 57, 59, 63
Americana, 35
Amish, 10
Army Issue, 10, 11
Army, Salvation, 48
Ashton, John, 20

Barbarians, 14
basque, 22
bazaars, 46, 51, 63, 79
belts, 13
bills, 20
British Exhibition, 23
Bryan, William Jennings, 90
bubble, 19
bugs, 42
button boxes, 27, 32, 48
button gardens, 59, 60, 61
"Buttons," 5
buttons: airplane, 39; ball, 82; bangers, 8; bone, 22; brass, 7, 21, 38; bronze, 7; campaign, 29, 37; calico, 23, 27; Centennial, 29; ceramic, 65; chased, 82; china, 23; Chinese, 72, 74; cloth, 20, 78; coins, 43; conventional, 37; crocheted, 11, 78; Dorset, 20; Dorset Wheel, 73, 75; drop, 20, 23; embroidered, 75, 76; engineers, 38; fancy, 23, 24; flat weave, 71, 72; foreign, 38, 43; gardens, 59; glass, 31; goofies, 37, 88; gold, 21, 87; hairpin lace, 77; handmade, 25, 79; horn, 22; ivory, 37, 83; materials, 11, 12, 185; metal, 7, 18, 22, 23, 82, 87; military, 28; motto, 31; overall, 37; pearl, 26, 31, 33, 61; pinbacks, 37, 52, 88, 89, 90; plate, 21; plastic (synthetic) 11, 12, 42, 69, 89; pottery, 11, 65, 66; realistics, 37; rebus, 31; repoussé, 32; ribbon, 70; roll-up, 71; shell, 22, 83; shankeys, 8; silver, 21, 29; sinkeys, 8; sports, 69, 86; trays, 40, 53; twist-apart, 10; uniform, 38; watches, 83; wood, 22
buttonwood, 5

cacti, 59
camlett, 21
cards, 62
carvings, 15
Casebolt, Florence, 59
Charm Strings, 27, 86, 87
Charms, 40, 42
Chinese gown, 10
churches, 15
clasps, 13
cloaks, 14, 16
coins, 43
collectors, 1, 3, 26, 38, 40, 48, 53, 86
Cooper Union, 66
Costermonger, 31, 32, 33, 47
cottage industry, 20
Croft, Henry, 32

decorations, wall, 57, 61
diamonds, 10, 20, 87
diaries, 20
di Bicci, Giovanni, 17
Dickinson, Charles, 6, 7,
disk, 14, 20
display, 48, 54
documents, 20
domes, 10
Dorset Buttons, 20
Dorset, East, 19, 20
dusters, linen, 38

Eisenhower, Dwight D., 90, 91
elephant, white, 46
Elinor, Queen, 16
embroidery, 15, 22
Emilio, Capt. Luis Fenolosa, 27, 28, 29
entomologists, 40
Essex Institute, 28

fairs: school, 46; church, 46
fashions, 16, 57, 62

fibulae, 13, 80
fines, 16
Florence, Italy, 17
flowers, 43
footpads, 18
fortune telling, 7
frames, 54, 57, 58
framing, 54, 55
fraternals, 86

Galloway, George Norton, 28
Glenn, John, 91
Godey's Ladies Book, 24
goldsmiths, 19
Grimes, Old, 12
guns, 48
Gwinnet, Button, 6

Hanna, Mark, 89
Harrison, Gen. Wm. Henry, 30
hats, 17
hoods, 14
hymn books, 15
4-H, 41

insects, 40
Iron Age, 14
Ives, 38

jackanapes, 21
Jackets, 31
Jackson, Andrew, 6, 11
jewelers, 19
Johnson, David F., 29

Kennedy, John F., 91
Kid, Yellow, 90
Kids, Katzenjammer, 90
knob, 14

laces, 22
laws, sumptuary, 18
letters, 20

Linley, Florence, 86
Lionel, 38
lists, laundry, 20
lists, shopping, 20
Liveries, 8

machine, button making, 20
manuscripts, 15
market, farmers, 49
McIntosh, Gen. Lachlan, 6
McKinley, William, 89
mementos, 43
Metropolitan Museum of Art, 68
missals, 15
mounting (display), 55, 56

National Button Society, 36, 88
National Geographic, 40
New York Exhibition of Industry, 23
newspapers, 20, 21, 43

O.K., 30
Overton, 6, 7
Oxford University, 84

pearls, 10, 83, 87
Pearly, King, Queen, 32, 33
Pendleton, Judge Charles, 30
pennies, pitching, 7
Pepys, Samuel, 21
poke boxes, 36
portraits, 22
pin-backs, 52, 81, 88, 89
pins, 13, 17, 80

Raleigh, Sir Walter, 83
repoussé, 82
rebuses, 31
ribbon, embroidered, 70
Richelieu, Cardinal, 84
Road to Ruin, 31
robbers, highway, 18
rubber, vulcanizing, 19

saints, 15
Schleswig, Denmark, 14
sculpture, church, 15
Sheffield, 19
shells, 43
shoes, 17, 86
shops: curio, 48; junk, 48; Japanese, 59, 60; second-hand, 48; tailor, 47; thrift, 48
smugglers, 10
Sobo, 61
stamps, 38, 42
stamps: airmail, 39; commemorative, 39; foreign, 39
State Flowers, 43
State Seals, 43
succulents, 60
suckling, 18

Urbana, Ohio, 30

Valentines, 42
varnish, 70
Victorian, 26
vulcanizing, 19

War of 1812, 22
Ward, Charlie L., 87
warriors, Scotch, 8
Washington, George, 29
watches, 83
weavers, 19
Whitehead & Hoag, 89
Willkie, Wendell, 90
wills, 20
wire: copper, 66, 67; gold, silver, 82
Women's Exchange, 51
Worcester, England, 21
World War I, 24, 87

zipper, 7